JEFFREY A. GILL

Christ Displays His Glory

Christ Displays His Glory

by
John MacArthur, Jr.

WORD OF GRACE COMMUNICATIONS
P.O. Box 4000
Panorama City, CA 91412

© 1987 by
JOHN F. MACARTHUR, JR.

All Scripture quotations, unless noted otherwise, are from the *New Scofield Reference Bible*, King James Version. Copyright © 1967 by Oxford University Press, Inc. Reprinted by permission.

Library of Congress Cataloging in Publication Data

MacArthur, John F.
  Christ displays his glory.

  (John MacArthur's Bible studies)
  Includes indexes.
    1. Bible. N.T. Matthew XVI, 24-XVII, 13—Criticism
interpretation, etc. I. Title. II. Series: MacArthur,
John F. Bible studies.
BS2575.2.M23   1987   226'.206   87-11117
ISBN 0-8024-5317-1

1 2 3 4 5 6 7 Printing/LC/Year 91 90 89 88 87

Printed in the United States of America

Contents

These Bible studies are taken from messages delivered by Pastor-Teacher John MacArthur, Jr., at Grace Community Church in Panorama City, California. These messages have been combined into a 4-tape album entitled *Christ Displays His Glory*. You may purchase this series either in an attractive vinyl cassette album or as individual cassettes. To purchase these tapes, request the album *Christ Displays His Glory*, or ask for the tapes by their individual GC numbers. Please consult the current price list; then, send your order, making your check payable to:

WORD OF GRACE COMMUNICATIONS
P.O. Box 4000
Panorama City, CA 91412

Or call the following number:
818-982-7000

1
Winning by Losing: The Paradox of Discipleship

Outline

Introduction
A. The Self-Centeredness of Contemporary Christianity
B. The Self-Sacrifice of True Christianity
   1. Matthew 10:37-39
   2. Mark 10:21
   3. Luke 14:25-27
   4. John 12:24-25

Lesson
I. The Principle (v. 24)
   A. Reiterating the Teaching on Commitment
      1. The affirmation of the disciples
         a) Great expectations
         b) Ultimate realization
      2. The authority of Christ
         a) In building His church
         b) In delegating His authority
      3. The attack of Satan
         a) Satan's favorite tool
         b) Peter's faulty mind-set
   B. Reaffirming the Terms of Commitment
      1. Dying to self
         a) The right perspective
            (1) Recognizing your inadequacy
            (2) Recognizing Christ's sufficiency
         b) The right attitude
            (1) Internal poverty
            (2) Desperate passion
         c) The right action

7

Introduction

Matthew 16:24-27 is our text for this lesson: "Then said Jesus unto his disciples, If any man will come after me, let him deny himself, and take up his cross, and follow me. For whosoever will save his life shall lose it; and whosoever will lose his life for my sake shall find it. For what is a man profited, if he shall gain the whole world, and lose his own soul? Or what shall a man give in exchange for his soul? For the Son of man shall come in the glory of his Father with his angels, and then he shall reward every man according to his works."

A. The Self-Centeredness of Contemporary Christianity

This passage strikes a deathblow to the current trend toward self-centered consumption in much of contemporary Christianity. Many people wish to identify themselves with Christianity only for what they can receive. They view Jesus as a utilitarian genie, fulfilling every whim. Some say Jesus wants to make you healthy, wealthy, and happy. If you are not all those things, then you supposedly don't have enough faith to appropriate what's yours. They claim Christianity is designed to give you everything you need and want. Even evangelicals and fundamentalists through the years have been guilty of propagating a Jesus who is a panacea for everything. Self-esteem promoters tell us Jesus came to boost our self-image. But they have fallen victim to narcissism—the pervasive self-love of contemporary society.

B. The Self-Sacrifice of True Christianity

Coming to Jesus Christ to receive material things is a prostitution of divine intention. It is true that when you come to Christ you receive and continue to receive blessings from Him. But there must be a cross before a crown, suffering before glory, and sacrifice before reward. That is what our Lord teaches in Matthew 16:24-27. We are to win by losing. Jesus taught His disciples that lesson many times.

1. Matthew 10:37-39—"He that loveth father or mother more than me, is not worthy of me; and he that loveth son or daughter more than me, is not worthy of me. And he that taketh not his cross and followeth after me, is not worthy of me. He that findeth his life shall lose it; and he that loseth his life for my sake shall find it."

2. Mark 10:21—"Jesus, beholding him [the rich young ruler], loved him, and said unto him, One thing thou lackest; go thy way, sell whatever thou hast, and give to the poor, and thou shalt have treasure in heaven; and come, take up the cross, and follow me."

3. Luke 14:25-27—"There went great multitudes with him [Christ]; and he turned, and said unto them, If any man come to me, and hate not his father, and mother, and wife, and children, and brethren, and sisters, yea, and his own life also, he cannot be my disciple. And whosoever doth not bear his cross, and come after me, cannot be my disciple."

4. John 12:24-25—Jesus said, "Except a grain of wheat fall into the ground and die, it abideth alone; but if it die, it bringeth forth much fruit. He that loveth his life shall lose it; and he that hateth his life in this world shall keep it unto life eternal."

Matthew 16:24-27 is a repeated principle. The apostle Paul said, "We must through much tribulation enter into the kingdom of God" (Acts 14:22). You will never understand what it means to be a disciple of Christ until you grasp the principle of winning by losing.

Lesson

I. THE PRINCIPLE (v. 24)

"Jesus said unto his disciples, If any man will come after me, let him deny himself, and take up his cross, and follow me."

A. Reiterating the Teaching on Commitment

In Matthew 8:20 Jesus tells a would-be disciple that "foxes have holes, and the birds of the air have nests, but the Son of man hath not where to lay his head." Jesus emphasized the cost involved in being His disciple. He talked about the pain involved, the need to sever certain relationships, the inevitable hostility, and the willingness to suffer. In Matthew 16:24-27 He reiterates that same teaching to His disciples. Why did He need to repeat it if He had taught it before? Because it was clear to Christ that they had not understood the lesson.

1. The affirmation of the disciples

    a) Great expectations

    The disciples had been raised with a specific understanding about the coming of the Messiah. They expected Him to overthrow the Roman yoke, dethrone the Herods, and establish the kingdom in all its glory. The longer Jesus delayed in doing so, the more difficult it became for them to wait. When Christ was given the opportunity to be made king, He fled (John 6:15). The people misunderstood Him. The religious leaders, instead of proclaiming Him as the Messiah, hated Him and sought to kill Him.

    b) Ultimate realization

    As the disciples spent two-and-a-half years with Jesus, they had no human explanation for His miracles

10

or His words. Because of God's work in their hearts, they finally came to the conclusion that Christ was the Messiah. That made them willing to wait. In Matthew 16:16 Peter affirms the consensus of all the disciples: "Thou art the Christ, the Son of the living God."

2. The authority of Christ

   a) In building His church

   In response Jesus said, "I will build my church, and the gates of Hades [a Hebrew term for death] shall not prevail against it" (v. 18). That means if the opposition took Christ's life, He would rise from the dead. It also means that if they took His disciples' lives, they too would rise. Death—to say nothing of anything in life—cannot contain the power of the church. What a glorious truth for the disciples to hear.

   b) In delegating His authority

   Then Jesus said, "I will give unto thee the keys of the kingdom of heaven; and whatsoever thou shalt bind [forbid] on earth [shall have been forbidden] in heaven; and whatsoever thou shalt loose [permit] on earth [shall have been permitted] in heaven" (v. 19). The apostles' decisions would reflect the will of God. Verse 17 explains how that could be possible: "Flesh and blood hath not revealed it unto thee, but my Father, who is in heaven."

The disciples learned that God would reveal His truth to them. They could see the glory of the Messiah, the gathering of the redeemed, and themselves as the heroes of the kingdom. It was a great moment for which they had waited a long time.

3. The attack of Satan

   a) Satan's favorite tool

   In verse 21 Jesus tells the disciples He will have to go to Jerusalem and be killed. The disciples never listened to what Jesus said after that; they heard only the shocking prophecy of His death. Verses 22-23 say, "Peter took him, and began to rebuke him, saying, Be it far from thee, Lord; this shall not be unto thee. But [Jesus] turned and said unto Peter, Get thee behind me, Satan." Jesus recognized the real attacker. Peter was merely a tool: Satan had been trying to divert Christ from the cross ever since he first tempted Him in the wilderness (Matt. 4:1-11).

   b) Peter's faulty mind-set

   In verse 23 Christ categorizes Peter's attitude: "Thou art an offense unto me; for thou savorest not the things that are of God, but those that are of men." Peter offended Christ because he was following a worldly train of thought. Men of the world want a reward without sacrifice. But according to God, the opposite is true. Whether incarnate in the Son or alive in the hearts of His people, God cannot exist in the midst of an anti-God society without generating some hostility. That's why 2 Timothy 3:12 says, "All that will live godly in Christ Jesus shall suffer persecution." Peter did not understand that holiness in the midst of an unholy society will create a negative reaction.

B. Reaffirming the Terms of Commitment

   Jesus knew He needed to remind His disciples of the first lesson He taught them. They were called to leave everything—family, livelihood, life-style, and home—to follow Him. So He told them, "If any man will come after me, let him deny himself, and take up his cross, and follow me" (v. 24).

   The phrase "if any man will come after me" is similar to the phrase "if you want to be a Christian." It is an evangelistic statement. But why would He say that to the disciples? Because the evangelistic thrust is to the multitude that also was present (Mark 8:34). Yet it was of tremendous value to the disciples. Having already made a commitment to Christ, we tend to do what we want when we are secure in Him and avoid the reproach that comes from being a good representative of Jesus Christ. If you want to follow Christ, you must do so on His terms. Like us, the disciples needed a reaffirmation of what those terms were.

What should our attitude be when coming to Christ? There are three factors to consider: dying to self, bearing the cross, and living in obedience.

1. Dying to self

   a) The right perspective

      (1) Recognizing your inadequacy

          Matthew 16:24 says, "Let him deny himself." The Greek word translated "deny" means "to disown." Verse 24 could be translated, "Let him refuse any association or companionship with himself." Jesus is not referring to your conscious self. You must reach the point where you are willing to deny that you have the capacity to save yourself or to be what God wants you to be. To come to Christ you must affirm that no good thing dwells in your flesh (Rom. 7:18), acknowledging that you contribute nothing to your redemption. The self-esteem cults that propagate love of self take people away from the message of the Bible. The more you love yourself the less likely you are to sense your need for a savior. To disown yourself is the first essential step in the Christian life. That's the way you come to Christ, and that's the way you continue to live.

      (2) Recognizing Christ's sufficiency

          A person must see his sin. He must see himself judged and condemned to hell, knowing he can do nothing of himself to change that outcome. In

13

desperation he must reach out and seek a rescuer outside of himself: Christ. Self is cast away when Christ enters in. The apostle Paul said, "I am crucified with Christ: nevertheless I live; yet not I, but Christ lives in me" (Gal. 2:20). He subjected himself to the lordship of Jesus Christ. Paul also said, "We . . . worship God in the spirit, and rejoice in Christ Jesus, and have no confidence in the flesh" (Phil. 3:3). When you come to Christ, you must do so on His terms: self-denial.

b) The right attitude

(1) Internal poverty

The greatest sermon ever preached on the subject of salvation is the Sermon on the Mount. In Matthew 5:3 Christ describes the attitude of those who will enter the kingdom: "Blessed are the poor in spirit; for theirs is the kingdom of heaven." Poverty of spirit is the foundation of virtue. The Greek word translated "poor" in verse 3 is *ptōchos*. It refers to someone so poor that he is forced to beg. Such a person is destitute, humbled by his wretched state. The Lord is saying that those who enter His kingdom know they have no resources of their own. Until we know how damned we are, we will never appreciate how precious Christ's forgiveness is. Until we know how utterly poor we are, we can never know how great His riches are. Out of the carcass comes the honey (Judg. 14:9), and out of deadness life is born. The psalmist said, "The Lord is near unto those who are of a broken heart, and saveth such as be of a contrite spirit" (Ps. 34:18).

(2) Desperate passion

Only desperate people come to God. In Luke 18:10 a tax collector and a Pharisee go into the Temple to pray. The Pharisee "prayed thus with himself, God, I thank thee that I am not as other men are . . . even as this tax collector. I fast twice

14

in the week; I give tithes of all that I possess" (vv. 11-12). He had an inflated self-image. The tax collector "would not lift up so much as his eyes unto heaven, but smote upon his breast, saying, God, be merciful to me a sinner" (v. 13). Jesus said, "This man went down to his house justified rather than the other" (v. 14). People will come to Christ when they have run out of resources—when they know they can't do anything about their sin. The intention of the Old Testament was to show men how unredeemable they are on their own terms. It is through grace alone that the sinner can know God through Christ.

c) The right action

According to Matthew 5:4 those who are poor in spirit mourn over their condition. They are also meek, knowing that nothing good is in them (v. 5). They therefore hunger and thirst for righteousness (v. 6)—something they desperately want but can't receive because it isn't within their grasp. As a result they are utterly dependent on God.

The broken sinner comes to Christ denying himself. The proud sinner wants both Christ and his pleasures, his covetousness, and his immorality. But he won't ever know Christ unless he comes on Christ's terms. Once a sinner has come to Christ, he is to live a life of self-denial. It is actually a happy way of life. I'm not happy when my self acts; I am happy when the Spirit of God acts through me. Joy comes through obedience and holiness. Bible scholar Arthur Pink said that growth in grace is a growth downward: it is the forming of a lower estimate of ourselves; it is a deepening realization of our nothingness; and it is a heartfelt recognition that we are not worthy of the least of God's mercies. Colossians 3:5 says we have to kill our fleshly desires. We have to put off our old man, which has been corrupted by lust (Eph. 4:22). An attitude of self-denial is crucial for entrance into the kingdom, and then it becomes the believer's life pattern. We say no to self and yes to the Spirit of God.

Living a Life of Self-Denial

An unknown author wrote about self-denial in this way: "Suppose you have been neglected or unforgiven. You sting with the hurt of the insult from such an oversight, but your heart is happy because you have been counted worthy to suffer for Christ. That is what dying to self is all about. When your wishes are crossed, your advice disregarded, and your opinions ridiculed, and yet you refuse to let anger rise in your heart or try to defend yourself, you are practicing dying to self. When you lovingly and patiently stand face to face with folly and spiritual insensitivity, and endure it as Jesus did, you have died to self. When you are content with any food, money, clothing, climate, society, solitude, or interruption by the will of God, you have died to self. When you never care to refer to yourself in conversation, record your own good works, or desire commendation from others, you are dying to self. When you can honestly rejoice with a brother who has prospered and had his needs met, and never feel any envy though your needs are greater and still unmet, you have practiced dying to self. When you can receive correction and reproof from one of less stature than yourself, and humbly admit he's right with no resentment or rebellion in your heart, you have died to self. Are you dead yet?"

2. Taking up the cross

   a) The willingness to suffer

   Taking up the cross refers to the willingness to endure persecution, rejection, reproach, shame, suffering, and even martyrdom for the sake of Christ.

   (1) As a common criminal

   What were the disciples thinking on that dusty road in Caesarea Philippi, two thousand years ago when Jesus said, "Take up [your] cross"? First-century Jewish historian Josephus tells us that eight hundred Jews were crucified in Jerusalem more than one hundred years before Christ's ministry (*Antiquities* 13.14.2). After a revolt following the death of Herod the Great in 4 B.C., the Roman proconsul Varus crucified two thousand

Jews (*Antiquities* 17.10.10). Crucifixion was a common practice in the Roman Empire.

When Jesus said, "Take up [your] cross," the disciples saw poor condemned souls marching along a road with the instrument of their own death strapped to their backs. Carrying one's cross meant walking to one's death. That's what the Lord wanted them to see. The disciples needed to perceive that following Christ was like carrying the instrument of their own execution. All but one of the eleven died as martyrs. Most of you won't be martyred, but you will bear reproach and ridicule if you live for Christ (2 Tim. 3:12). You must be willing to suffer the indignities of a condemned criminal in service to Christ should you be called to do so.

(2) As an associate of Christ

In our day we are not being martyred for our obedience to Christ, but we still must bear reproach. Practicing self-denial means identifying with Christ and naming His name up to and including the point of death. Most of us would say, "If I ever got to that point, I don't think I could handle it." But if you ever face that situation, 1 Peter 4:14 says, "the Spirit of glory and of God resteth upon you." You would have such an overwhelming sense of God's grace that you would find great joy in the midst of your situation.

Coming to Christ is not just a matter of signing on the dotted line or raising your hand. When you are enamored by the precious gift of salvation through Christ, you will sacrifice even your self. After receiving Christ's gift, isn't it amazing how we back off from that original commitment? That's why Christ reminded the disciples as well as instructed the crowd about their commitment.

(*a*) Matthew 10:24-25—Jesus said, "The disciple is not above his teacher, nor the servant above

17

his lord. It is enough for the disciple that he be like his teacher, and the servant like his lord." He warned His disciples that they would be persecuted (v. 23).

(b) Matthew 10:34-36—Jesus continued, "Think not that I am come to send peace on earth; I came not to send peace, but a sword. For I am come to set a man at variance against his father, and the daughter against her mother, and the daughter-in-law against her mother-in-law. And a man's foes shall be they of his own household."

Hostility results when godliness invades ungodliness. Yet there is a marvelous ambivalence in that truth. Although it is true the world despises us, it can't help but be attracted to us at the same time. However, the emphasis in Matthew 16:24 is on the reproach. The cross indicates our suffering because of our connection to Jesus Christ. Picture Jesus Christ moving along the road to His execution, bearing on His back the cross on which He will bear the sins of all the world. Following Him are millions, all bearing their crosses, willing to share in His sufferings. What a glorious scene! You're not called to Christ to receive blessing; you're called to abandon yourself in service to Him. A willingness to bear one's cross is the mark of a true disciple. A good test to separate the wheat from the tares (Matt. 13:24-30, 36-43) is to see who is willing to suffer the reproach of Christ. The tares won't pay that kind of price.

b) The way of life

Luke 9:23 says, "Take up [your] cross *daily*" (emphasis added). Self-sacrifice is a way of life for us. In the hymn "Must Jesus Bear the Cross Alone?" eighteenth-century lyricist Thomas Shepherd said,

> Must Jesus bear the cross alone
> And all the world go free?
> No, there's a cross for ev'ry one,
> And there's a cross for me.

The consecrated cross I'll bear
Till death shall set me free,
And then go home my crown to wear,
For there's a crown for me.

3. Living in obedience

Matthew 16:24 says, "And follow me." The text literally says, "Let him be following me." Being a disciple of Christ becomes a pattern of living. We are to imitate Christ. If we say we belong to Jesus, we ought "to walk, even as he walked" (1 John 2:6). We need to be obedient to the divine will. That's what our Lord meant when He said, "Not every one that saith unto me, Lord, Lord, shall enter into the kingdom of heaven, but he that doeth the will of my Father, who is in heaven" (Matt. 7:21).

The true disciple is marked by dying to self, taking up the cross, and living in obedience. In John 8:31 Jesus says, "If ye continue in my word, then are ye my disciples indeed." If you were going to take a trip, the first thing you'd do is say good-bye and pick up your bags. The second thing you'd do is proceed on your trip. The same applies here. You say good-bye to self, pick up your burden (your cross), and follow in loyal obedience.

II. THE PARADOX (vv. 25-26)

A. The Eternal Choices (v. 25)

"Whosoever will save his life shall lose it; and whosoever will lose his life for my sake shall find it."

Whoever lives only to preserve his earthly comforts will lose his eternal soul. But whoever is willing to deny himself and follow Christ will save his soul. You have a choice. The Greek word here translated "life" is frequently translated elsewhere as "soul" or "self." Christ is referring to your soul, the internal part of you.

A willingness to pay the price may mean martyrdom, as in the case of Paul. It may mean sickness, as in the case of Epaphroditus (Phil. 2:25-27). It's not likely to mean martyrdom in our day, but if a person truly follows Jesus Christ, he must be willing to abandon his own security and comfort.

Willing to Pay the Price

A story is told of a slave who was always happy and singing. One day his master asked what made him that way. The slave said, "I love the Lord Jesus Christ because He has forgiven my sin. And that puts a song in my heart." The master asked how he could have what the slave had. The slave replied, "Go put on your white suit and come down here and work in the mud with us. Then you can have what I have." The master refused and rode away. But later he came back because he admired the slave's attitude toward life. After asking the same question and receiving the same answer, the master rode off in a huff. Some weeks later he returned again and said in desperation that he would do what the slave said. The slave replied, "Good! Then you don't have to. You only had to be willing to do it."

I'm not saying God will make you a martyr. But if you come to Jesus Christ on His terms, you had better be willing to be a martyr if God so chooses. Be willing to lose your life to gain eternal life. Don't try to preserve your life on earth at all costs and therefore forfeit eternal life.

  B. The Eternal Questions (v. 26)

    1. Can you profit from the world? (v. 26*a*)

      "What is a man profited [lit., "what use is it for a man"], if he shall gain the whole world, and lose his own soul?"

      That is the ultimate hyperbole. Suppose a man owns everything on the earth but loses his soul. What does he have? Nothing. What good is it for a dead man to own anything?

    2. Can you buy your soul? (v. 26*b*)

      "What shall a man give in exchange for his soul?"

Could the dead man who owned the whole world buy back his soul with the world? No. If you throw your life away in this world, you will be bankrupt forever. But if you abandon your life and give it to Jesus Christ, you'll be rich forever. And He may choose to pour out some of those riches on you in this life as well.

III. THE *PAROUSIA* (Gk., "coming"; v. 27)

"The Son of man shall come in the glory of his Father with his angels, and then he shall reward every man according to his works."

There is coming a day when the Judge will arrive. John 5:27 says the Father has given the Son all authority to execute judgment. When Christ says, "He shall reward every man according to his works" (Matt. 16:27), He is not referring to salvation by works. We are not saved by our works, but we are judged by our works (Rom. 2). We read that believers are judged on the basis of what they do because that reveals who they are (1 Cor. 3:11-15). The phrase "shall come" means "about to come." That is the first indication of the second coming in the New Testament.

No one will escape the final judgment of God. Psalm 62:12 says, "O Lord . . . thou renderest to every man according to his work." Romans 14:12 says, "So, then, every one of us shall give account of himself to God." In the day of reckoning, God will look at a man's works and say, "There's a believer; I can tell by his works. They are the product of the Spirit. There's an unbeliever; I can tell by his works. They're the product of the flesh." Works are the objective criteria by which God can evaluate the subjective reality of a man's faith.

God's judgment is twofold. Luke emphasizes the shame the ungodly will feel (Luke 9:26). They will be judged according to their works and sent to hell. Believers also will be judged, but they will be rewarded according to their works. We will receive crowns if we have been faithful.

Jesus is saying to the crowd, "You had better give up your life, take up your cross, and follow Me. If you don't, a day is coming when you'll be cast into hell." To the disciples He is saying, "You'd better be faithful to deny yourself, take up your cross, and live in obedience, because a day is coming when you'll be rewarded." The man who selfishly clings to his life—whose overwhelming concern is comfort, security, prosperity, and self-indulgence—is an eternal pauper. The man who gives his life for Christ—who abandons himself to the will of God—will be with God forever. Only a fool struggles with that kind of choice. Nevertheless, there will be those who, as in Jeremiah's day, forsake "the fountain of living waters, and [hew] out cisterns, broken cisterns, that can hold no water" (Jer. 2:13).

Focusing on the Facts

1. What has happened to much of contemporary Christianity (see p. 8)?
2. What must Christians experience before they are rewarded (see p. 9)?
3. Why did Jesus need to repeat the lesson in Matthew 16:24-27 to the disciples (see p. 10)?
4. What did the disciples expect from Jesus (see p. 10)?
5. What two things did Christ say He would do in response to Peter's declaration (Matt. 16:16-18; see p. 11)?
6. What did Satan attempt to do through the rebuke of Peter (Matt. 16:21-23; see p. 12)?
7. Why did Peter offend Christ with his rebuke (Matt. 16:23; see p. 12)?
8. For what two reasons did Christ make an evangelistic statement to the disciples in Matthew 16:24 (see pp. 12-13)?
9. What are three factors to consider in coming to Christ (see p. 13)?
10. Explain what Christ meant when He said, "Let him deny himself" (see p. 13)?
11. How must the heart of man see itself (see p. 13)?
12. According to Matthew 5:3, what kind of attitude is necessary to enter the kingdom of heaven (see p. 14)?
13. Explain what it means to die to self (see p. 16).
14. What does it mean to take up one's cross? What significance did it have for the disciples (see pp. 16-17)?
15. In what way does God allow a believer to find joy in the midst of dying because of his identification with Christ (1 Pet. 4:14; see p. 17)?
16. How often must a believer take up his cross? Why (see p. 18)?

17. What should be the pattern of a believer's life (1 John 2:6; see p. 19)?
18. What will happen to those who seek to preserve their comfort and self-indulgence (Matt. 16:25; see p. 19)?

Pondering the Principles

1. Do you find that as a believer you have a tendency to demand back some of your rights as a result of the security you have in Christ? Are you avoiding the reproach and hostility you would receive by being openly associated with Christ? Remember the attitude you had when you came to Christ for salvation. Read Matthew 5:3-6. Which of those attitudes do you need to cultivate again in your life? Prayerfully consider how God would want you to implement each one into your life today.

2. Review the section "Living a Life of Self-Denial" (p. 16). How many of those statements have been or are true of you? How many have you experienced but failed to endure to the end? Those examples illustrate how hard it is for us to die to self. Perhaps you are experiencing a situation that is similar to one of those listed. What must you do in that situation to practice dying to self? Know that the Holy Spirit will back up your commitment to obey God. Thank God for that assurance.

3. Read 1 Peter 4:12-19. According to verses 13, 16, and 19, what should a believer do when he suffers? According to verse 14, what kind of attitude should a believer adopt when he is reproached for the name of Christ? How is he able to do that? The next time you suffer as a Christian, read this passage, and follow what it says. You will find yourself blessed because of your obedience.

4. Are you willing to pay the price of being a disciple of Christ? Examine your heart. Is there anything that might be preventing you from making a 100 percent commitment to Christ? If there is, confess it right now, and eliminate it from your life. If called on to do the most distasteful job you can think of, would you do it if it meant you identified yourself with Christ? If you can answer yes honestly, you are willing to pay the price.

2
A Preview of the Second Coming—Part 1

Outline

Introduction

Review
I. The Principle (16:24)
II. The Paradox (16:25-26)
III. The *Parousia* (16:27)

Lesson
  A. The Glory of the Prophecy
     1. Affirming the prophets
     2. Encouraging the disciples
  B. The Character of the Prophecy
     1. As a promise
        a) To all believers
        b) To the disciples
           (1) The conditions of discipleship
           (2) The compassion of the Lord
     2. As a warning
  C. The Particulars of the Prophecy
     1. The context of Christ's coming
        a) The primary prophecy in Daniel
           (1) The throne of judgment
           (2) The dominion of the Son
        b) The parallel prophecy in Matthew
     2. The character of Christ's glory
        a) Christ's deity veiled
        b) Christ's deity revealed
           (1) Exodus 33:18-19
           (2) Matthew 24:29-31

3. The criteria of Christ's judgment
   a) The purpose of works
      (1) To verify salvation
      (2) To manifest commitment
         (a) A righteous heart
         (b) An unrighteous heart
   b) The result of works
      (1) The promise
      (2) The warning
D. The Inadequacy of the Prophecy
IV. The Preview (16:28–17:13)
   A. The Promise of the Preview (16:28)
      1. Interpreted
         a) The incorrect interpretations
         b) The correct interpretation
      2. Internalized
         a) By Peter
         b) By John

Conclusion

Introduction

Matthew 16:27–17:13 is one of the highlights of the life of our Lord Jesus Christ and His disciples. The sixteenth chapter of Matthew contains some monumental realities. At this point in Christ's ministry it is just a few months until His death. As He moves toward it, He senses a great need to prepare His disciples for what they're going to endure in His death, resurrection, and ascension and their subsequent ministry. In the span of Matthew 16:16-28, He reveals to them that He is the Messiah, that He is building His kingdom, and that He will die, rise, and finally come again.

Review

I. THE PRINCIPLE (16:24; see pp. 10-19)

II. THE PARADOX (16:25-26; see pp. 19-21)

III. THE *PAROUSIA* (16:27; see pp. 21-22)

"For the Son of man shall come in the glory of his Father with his angels, and then he shall reward every man according to his works."

Lesson

Verse 27 is the first clear revelation in the life of our Lord of His second coming. His deity, death, resurrection, and eventual return constitute His instruction for the disciples in the few short months before His death. Even though the disciples would hear those lessons again and again, the message didn't sink in until after Christ was gone. The lessons then took on a deeper meaning than when the disciples first heard them.

A. The Glory of the Prophecy

1. Affirming the prophets

   The message that the Messiah would come in glory was not new. The Old Testament is filled with prophecies of it. The Davidic covenant promised there would come a King with an everlasting, glorious kingdom (2 Sam. 7:12-13, 16). Jesus was merely affirming to the disciples the glory the prophets said would come to pass through the Messiah.

2. Encouraging the disciples

   The disciples may have lost a sense of the Messiah's glory because of what had occurred in the life of Christ. To date He had not operated according to their messianic expectations. So the Lord added this significant dimension: the last view the world will have of Jesus Christ is not as a crucified criminal but as One coming again in full glory. The first time He came He received rejection and hostility and was executed as a criminal. The second time He will come in glory, majesty, dominion, power, and might as King of kings and Lord of lords. The hymn "Son of Man to Thee I Cry" says:

He who wept above the grave,
He who stilled the raging wave,
Meek to suffer, strong to save,
He shall come in glory.

He who sorrow's pathway trod,
He that ever good bestowed—
Son of Man and Son of God—
He shall come in glory.

He who bled with scourging sore,
Thorns and scarlet meekly wore,
He who every sorrow bore,
He shall come in glory.

Monarch of the smitten cheek,
Scorn of Jew and scorn of Greek,
Priest and king, divinely meek,
He shall come in glory.

He who died to set us free,
He who lives and loves even me,
He who comes, whom I shall see,
Jesus only—only He—
He shall come in glory.

That is a perspective the disciples needed because the messianic plan wasn't unfolding the way they expected.

B. The Character of the Prophecy

Matthew 16:27 needs to be seen from two vantage points.

1. As a promise

   a) To all believers

   Verse 27 is a promise to those who believe. The thought of His coming is a promise that fills us with great hope and anticipation. Like John we say, "Even so, come, Lord Jesus" (Rev. 22:20). We are like those who gather under the altar of God and cry out, "How long, O Lord, holy and true, dost thou not judge and

avenge our blood on them that dwell on the earth?"
(Rev. 6:10).

b) To the disciples

(1) The conditions of discipleship

In Matthew 16:24 Jesus gives the disciples the
conditions of discipleship. If anyone wants to be
a Christian—to identify with Him and enter His
kingdom—he must deny himself, bear his cross,
and follow in obedience. Self-denial implies sacrifice—saying no to self and yes to God. We must
say no to ease and comfort and yes to a cross—a
cross of rejection, persecution, and alienation
from the people of the world. It is a cross we
must carry willingly. Finally, we must say yes to
loyal obedience at any price.

It is easy to see how excited the disciples must
have been when they realized Christ was the
Messiah and heard Him say, "I will build my
church, and the gates of hades shall not prevail
against it. And I will give unto thee the keys of
the kingdom of heaven" (Matt. 16:18-19). I'm
sure they were thinking Christ was going to ush-
er in the kingdom right away. But then Christ
said "he must go unto Jerusalem, and suffer
. . . and be killed" (Matt. 16:21). Then He said,
"If any man will come after me, let him deny
himself, and take up his cross, and follow me"
(Matt. 16:24). Those were some strong realities
for the disciples to comprehend. They could see a
lot of suffering but not much glory.

(2) The compassion of the Lord

The Lord understood the disciples' frustration.
He never gives any of us more than we can bear.
So He said, "The Son of man shall come in the
glory of his Father with his angels" (Matt. 16:27).
The divine plan hadn't changed—it was still on
schedule. Later, the apostle Paul added a foot-
note to that when he said, "The sufferings of this

29

present time are not worthy to be compared with the glory which shall be revealed in us" (Rom. 8:18). Matthew 16:27 is filled with promise for the disciples and for us because we, like them, long for the coming of Jesus Christ.

2. As a warning

In Matthew 16:25 Jesus says, "Whosoever will save his life shall lose it." If you try to hang onto this world, you will forfeit eternity. In verse 26 He says, "What is a man profited, if he shall gain the whole world, and lose his own soul?" Verse 27 implies a similar warning: What about the people who do not belong to Jesus Christ—who never abandoned themselves, took up the cross, and followed Him? Verse 27 says, "He shall reward every man according to his works." The Christian eagerly awaits Christ's reappearance because he knows it is a time of reward. The non-Christian vigorously denies or dreads His appearance because he knows it is a time of judgment.

In the vision recorded in Revelation 10:8-11 the apostle John eats the title deed to the earth, which represents the coming of Jesus Christ. He said, "It was in my mouth sweet as honey, and as soon as I had eaten it my belly was bitter" (v. 10). The sweetness is the promise to believers; the bitterness is the warning to the unbelievers. Paul viewed the coming of Christ in the same way. He longed for Jesus to come, yet wrote, "Knowing, therefore, the terror of the Lord, we persuade men" (2 Cor. 5:11). So we rejoice because Jesus is coming, yet we are sad for those who don't know Him.

For some, Jesus' return will end a life of dying to self, taking up the cross, and living in obedience and will bring about eternal rest, riches, and prosperity. For others it will bring an end to a life of self-centeredness and self-indulgence, replaced by an eternity of torment, unrest, poverty, and loneliness. Jesus is not discussing any one element of the second coming; He is saying in verse 27 that when He comes, everyone will be dealt with. Before Christ's return the believers are raptured and immediately taken to the judgment seat of Christ, where they receive reward for

good they did through the Spirit of God. After His return
the unbelievers are ultimately gathered from out of the
land and sea and brought before the great white throne.
God as judge then sends them into the second death of everlasting hell. All those elements of judgment are general-
ized in Matthew 16:27.

C. The Particulars of the Prophecy

1. The context of Christ's coming

Verse 27 says that "the Son of man shall come." Why
does Jesus call Himself the Son of Man? He used that
identification more commonly than any other. It marks
His humanness—Jesus was God incarnate. But in the
context of verse 27 it has a richer meaning.

a) The primary prophecy in Daniel

Beginning at Daniel 7:9, Daniel is looking across the
history of the world to its conclusion—all the way to
final judgment.

(1) The throne of judgment

Daniel 7:9 says, "I beheld till the thrones were
placed, and the Ancient of days did sit, whose
garment was white as snow, and the hair of his
head like pure wool; his throne was like the fiery
flame, and his wheels as burning fire." God, who
is the Ancient of days, sits in judgment. His garment, white as snow, speaks of His purity. His
hair, like pure wool, refers to His wisdom. His
throne, like a fiery flame, refers to His majesty.
The whirling flames at the foot of the throne represent God's consuming judgment.

Verse 10 says, "A fiery stream issued and came
forth from before him." Judgment issuing from
the throne consumes everything in its path.
Verse 10 continues, "A thousand thousands min-
istered unto him, and ten thousand times ten
thousand [the angelic hosts] stood before him;
the judgment was set, and the books were

opened." God's final accounting will be based on objective data. He keeps records, and He will look at them on Judgment Day.

(2) The dominion of the Son

Verses 11-12 describe the destruction of the Beast—the satanic world leader. Then in verses 13-14 Daniel says, "I saw in the night visions, and, behold, one like the Son of man came with the clouds of heaven, and came to the Ancient of days, and they brought him near before him. And there was given him dominion, and glory, and a kingdom, that all people, nations, and languages should serve him; his dominion is an everlasting dominion, which shall not pass away, and his kingdom that which shall not be destroyed." The Son of Man will come in glory to receive the kingdom and to act in harmony with the Father in judgment.

b) The parallel prophecy in Matthew

Matthew 16:27 is a prophecy similar to Daniel 7:13-14 in that it portrays Jesus as the Son of Man returning to judge men on behalf of God. He will take those who belong to Him into His glorious kingdom, and those who don't belong to Him will be thrown out of the kingdom forever (Matt. 25:46).

2. The character of Christ's glory

Matthew 16:27 says Christ will "come in the glory of his Father." The word *glory* is one way to express the attributes, nature, and character of God. Jesus will come as a blazing manifestation of the eternal God.

a) Christ's deity veiled

When Jesus came into the world, His deity was veiled. He was among men, but most didn't know who He was. They didn't receive Him. They saw no beauty in Him that they should desire Him (Isa. 53:2).

b) Christ's deity revealed

When Christ returns the veil will be pulled back, and He will come in the glory of His unveiled Father. There will be a full display of His divine attributes.

(1) Exodus 33:18-19—Moses said to God, "Show me thy glory" (v. 18). God replied, "I will make all my goodness pass before thee, and I will proclaim the name of the Lord before thee, and will be gracious to whom I will be gracious, and will show mercy on whom I will show mercy" (v. 19). Moses wanted to see God's glory, so God showed Moses His attributes (grace and mercy, in this case). God's glory is His attributes. God's glory is the manifestation of all He is in holiness.

(2) Matthew 24:29-31—Jesus said that "immediately after the tribulation . . . shall the sun be darkened, and the moon shall not give its light, and the stars shall fall from heaven, and the powers of the heavens shall be shaken" (v. 29). Revelation 6:14 says, "The heaven departed as a scroll when it is rolled together," as blinds might roll up when they slip from your hand. Matthew 24:30-31 says, "Then shall appear the sign of the Son of man in heaven; and then shall all the tribes of the earth mourn, and they shall see the Son of man coming in the clouds of heaven with power and great glory. And he shall send his angels with a great sound of a trumpet."

Christ will return in the blazing, unveiled glory of God, lighting the whole universe. Men will scream and try to hide from His light. The Bible says that when He touches the earth His glory will fill the earth (Zech. 14:7). He will establish His kingdom, and we will dwell with Him in glory. But those who refuse the Savior will be cast out from His presence forever.

3. The criteria of Christ's judgment

Matthew 16:27 says that when Christ comes, He will "reward every man according to his works." On what basis will His judgment be made? On the basis of works. Many people misunderstand what Christ is saying here. They note that Ephesians 2:8-9 says, "By grace are ye saved through faith; and that not of yourselves, it is the gift of God—not of works, lest any man should boast." Yes, we are saved by faith, but that is a different issue. Scripture also teaches that God will judge all men on the basis of their deeds (e.g., Rom. 2:5-11; 1 Cor. 3:8, 12-13; 2 Cor. 5:10; Gal. 6:7-8; Rev. 2:23; 20:12; 22:12). Romans 14:12 says, "Every one of us shall give account of himself to God."

a) The purpose of works

(1) To verify salvation

When Jesus comes in judgment, He "will render to every man according to his deeds" (Rom. 2:6). The point is this: your knowledge of Jesus Christ must be evidenced by your good deeds. Works are not the basis of your salvation, but they are the objective verification that you are saved. James said, "Faith without works is dead" (James 2:20). The Lord revealed that truth in Matthew 7:21: "Not every one that saith unto me, Lord, Lord, shall enter into the kingdom of heaven, but he that doeth the will of my Father, who is in heaven." On Judgment Day, God will use objective criteria to verify the faith of the redeemed. Those who do not know Jesus Christ as Savior will have no righteous deeds accredited to them because God isn't alive in them to produce them. But God dwells in those who are saved through the Holy Spirit. He produces the good works that prove the transaction really occurred.

(2) To manifest commitment

(*a*) A righteous heart

Romans 2:7 says, "To them who by patient continuance in well-doing seek for glory and honor and immortality, eternal life." Those who pursue righteousness and seek heavenly

34

glory will receive eternal life. We know that no one will seek such things unless God has regenerated his heart. Romans 3:10-11 says, "There is none righteous, no, not one: there is none that understandeth, there is none that seeketh after God." The person who pursues righteousness and seeks glory in God's kingdom gives evidence that Christ has changed his heart.

(b) An unrighteous heart

Romans 2:8-11 says, "But unto them that are contentious, and do not obey the truth, but obey unrighteousness, indignation and wrath, tribulation and anguish, upon every soul of man that doeth evil, of the Jew first, and also of the Greek; but glory, honor, and peace, to every man that worketh good, to the Jew first, and also to the Greek; for there is no respect of persons with God."

God doesn't whimsically send people into heaven or hell. A person will enter the kingdom only if he belongs there on the basis of Christ's finished work—but his works will be evident.

b) The result of works

(1) The promise

Matthew 16:27 is a promise to those who love Christ. When I look at my life, I have to admit that I fail a lot. And you can say the same thing about your Christian life. Sometimes failure is all we see, and it's hard to find anything good. Then once you find something you did that you think was good, you have just corrupted it—you've injected pride into what originally was a humble act. We all struggle with that. But I have hope because I've given my heart to Jesus Christ, and I know He is producing through me works worthy of God's reward. When I stand before God, the record will show there is evidence in the life of John MacArthur that God changed his heart.

(2) The warning

No matter how good you may think you are, your goodness is not produced by God unless God lives in you. You can stand before God and say, "I did all these things in your name," but He will say, "I never knew you" (Matt. 7:22-23). For the unbeliever, that will be a day of great fear. The best description of it is given by the apostle Paul in 2 Thessalonians 1:5-10: "This is a manifest token of the righteous judgment of God, that ye may be counted worthy of the kingdom of God, for which ye also suffer, seeing it is a righteous thing with God to recompense tribulation to them that trouble you; and to you who are troubled, rest with us, when the Lord Jesus shall be revealed from heaven with his mighty angels, in flaming fire taking vengeance on them that know not God, and that obey not the gospel of our Lord Jesus Christ; who shall be punished with everlasting destruction from the presence of the Lord, and from the glory of his power, when he shall come to be glorified in his saints." The saints can rest because their glory is coming, and unbelievers must fear because vengeance is coming.

D. The Inadequacy of the Prophecy

The prophecy of Christ's second coming was a great encouragement to the disciples, but Christ knew they needed more. They were overwhelmed by their present situation. Their plan wasn't turning out as they hoped. After a brief moment when Christ said He would build His church and give them the keys to the kingdom of heaven, He announced He would die (Matt. 16:18-21). Next He rebuked Peter by saying, "Get thee behind me, Satan" (v. 23). Then He told them they needed to be willing to bear a cross and die for Him. All they could envision was hundreds of people walking to their own execution. The things they learned that day were difficult to comprehend. They were not the kinds of things they had expected when they chose to follow Christ. So when Christ told them that glory would come, you can imagine their thinking, *Sure it will!* The prophecy was too remote for them because of their present circumstances. We are like that. We become drowned in the present and view the second coming as an event somewhere off in the distant future. But that perception robs us of the purifying hope that the reality of Christ's return should create in us (1 John 3:3).

To counteract the disciples' frustration, the Lord illustrates His return in a dramatic and unforgettable way. He goes one step further with them because He knows their faith is weak.

IV. THE PREVIEW (16:28–17:13)

A. The Promise of the Preview (16:28)

"Verily I say unto you, There are some standing here, who shall not taste of death, till they see the Son of man coming in his kingdom."

1. Interpreted

That verse could lead you to believe that somewhere in this world are some extremely old men! What does Christ mean? I believe what Christ was saying can be translated, "Some of you standing here will see the Son of Man coming in His royal majesty before you die." The Greek word translated "kingdom" (*basileia*) is used more than 160 times in the New Testament. It is correct to render it not only as "kingdom" but also as "the kingliness of the King," "regal splendor," or "royal majesty." The emphasis in verse 28 is on the coming of the King Himself in His royal majesty.

a) The incorrect interpretations

Some commentators have suggested that Christ was referring to the resurrection—that He would come out of the grave in royal splendor. Some suggest He was referring to the coming of the Holy Spirit on the Day of Pentecost—that the Spirit would come in majesty at the birth of the church. Others say He was referring to the destruction of Jerusalem in A.D. 70, when He judged apostate Israel. Some have even suggested He was referring to a spiritual coming— that Christ enters your heart in regal splendor. It is true that all those things happened, but they don't have anything to do with Matthew 16:28. He couldn't have been referring to the resurrection because it is never expressed by the verb translated "coming." The resurrection is the first step in Christ's ascension to heaven, not His coming from heaven. He couldn't have been referring to Pentecost because the Holy Spirit, not Christ, came then. He couldn't have been referring to the destruction of Jerusalem because He said, "*Some of you* will see the Son of man" (emphasis added), and no one recorded seeing Him at the destruction. Finally, there is no justification for a mystical interpretation of verse 28 because the following context makes clear the meaning of the verse.

b) The correct interpretation

Unfortunately a chapter break was made by the translators at a point where it is important to follow the flow of the text. This same promise in Matthew 16:28 also appears in Mark and Luke. In all three cases it is immediately followed by the same incident, but in Mark (9:1-13) and Luke (9:27-36) it is not followed by a chapter break. What the Lord was referring to in Matthew 16:28 is interpreted by the event that follows. Three of the disciples were about to have a private showing of Christ's glory.

An Overview of the Transfiguration

Matthew 17:1 says, "After six days Jesus taketh Peter, James, and John, his brother." Those were the three who saw Christ in His regal splendor before their deaths. Matthew's narrative continues, "[Jesus] bringeth them up into an high mountain privately, and was transfigured before them; and his face did shine like the sun, and His raiment was as white as the light" (vv. 1-2). God flipped a switch and turned on deity from within Christ! To add to this scene "there appeared unto them Moses and Elijah talking with him. Then answered Peter, and said unto Jesus, Lord, it is good for us to be here; if thou wilt, let us make here three booths; one for thee, and one for Moses, and one for Elijah. While he yet spoke, behold, a bright cloud overshadowed them; and, behold, a voice out of the cloud, which said, This is my beloved Son, in whom I am well pleased; hear ye him. And when the disciples heard it, they fell on their face, and were very much afraid. And Jesus came and touched them, and said, Arise, and be not afraid. And when they had lifted up their eyes, they saw no man, except Jesus only" (vv. 3-8).

What an experience! The three disciples accompanied Jesus on a little retreat up the mountain. Luke says they were sleeping and Jesus was praying (Luke 9:29, 32). During the prayer and just as the disciples were coming out of their sleep, Jesus pulled back the veil and gave them a display of the glory He had promised them. They were terrified. And add to that the voice of God and the presence of Moses and Elijah! They were overwhelmed. What the disciples saw was a preview of the second coming. Every single detail of the preview depicts an element of the second coming.

2. Internalized

a) By Peter

That preview changed Peter's life. Don't worry about your pain or suffering; Jesus is coming—that became the theme of his epistles. The one thing Peter knew Jesus would do was return, and the resurrection verified it. He regressed some when Jesus died, but he was strengthened by the resurrection. The second coming became his great anticipation. I believe he was consumed with it. In 2 Peter 1:16-18 he says, "We have not followed cunningly devised fables when we made known unto you the power and coming of our Lord Jesus Christ, but were eyewitnesses of his majesty. For he received from God, the Father, honor and glory, when there came such a voice to him from the excellent glory, This is my beloved Son, in whom I am well pleased. And this voice which came from heaven we heard, when we were with him in the holy mount." When Peter preached about the second coming, he wasn't talking about something he hoped would happen; he knew it would happen because he had a preview of it.

b) By John

In John 1:14 John says, "The Word was made flesh, and dwelt among us (and we beheld his glory, the glory as of the only begotten of the Father), full of grace and truth."

Peter and John saw the partially unveiled glory of God in the transfiguration, and they wrote about it. James didn't write about it that we know of, but I'm sure he talked about it.

Conclusion

The Lord is gracious. He didn't just say He was going to come; He gave a preview of what His coming would be like. He encouraged Moses similarly, proclaiming, "It shall come to pass, while my glory passeth by, that I will put thee in a cleft of the rock, and will cover thee with my hand while I pass by; and I will take away mine hand, and thou shalt see my back; but my face shall not be seen" (Ex. 33:22-23). Moses then was assured God would lead him.

Christ didn't display His glory for the three disciples' benefit only: it was for our benefit as well. In 2 Peter 3:3-7 Peter says, "Knowing this first, that there shall come in the last days scoffers, walking after their own lusts, and saying, Where is the promise of his coming? For since the fathers fell asleep, all things continue as they were from the beginning of creation. For this they willingly are ignorant of, that by the word of God the heavens were of old, and the earth standing out of the water and in the water, by which the world that then was, being overflowed with water, perished. But the heavens and the earth which are now, by the same word are kept in store, reserved unto fire against the day of judgment and perdition of ungodly men." Peter concludes that in knowing all these things, "What manner of persons ought ye to be in all holy living and godliness?" (v. 11). Jesus is coming. What kind of person ought you to be? You will be judged by your works. God is keeping records, and there is no escape. For those of us who love the Lord Jesus Christ, there is sweetness in His coming. It is a promise filled with hope. But for those who do not know Jesus Christ, there will be terror and anguish.

Focusing on the Facts

1. Explain how the disciples could have lost a sense of the Messiah's future glory (see p. 27).
2. From what two perspectives can Matthew 16:27 be viewed (see pp. 28-30)?
3. Why was Matthew 16:27 so crucial for the disciples to hear (see pp. 29-30)?
4. Explain the significance Matthew 16:27 has for unbelievers (see p. 30).
5. Why does Jesus refer to Himself as the Son of Man in Matthew 16:27 (see p. 31)?
6. Daniel 7:9 gives a description of God. What attributes are symbolized in that description (see p. 31)?
7. How is Matthew 16:27 similar to the prophecy in Daniel 7:13-14 (see p. 32)?
8. What word can be used to express the attributes, nature, and character of God (see p. 32)?
9. Why didn't most of the world recognize Christ's deity when He first came to earth? How will they recognize His deity when He returns (see pp. 32-33)?
10. What is the criteria God will use when He judges all men (see Matt. 16:27)? Cite some verses that support that fact (see pp. 33-34).
11. Why does God use this criteria in His judgment of man (see pp. 34-35)?
12. Explain how the Christian can have hope in his ultimate reward despite the failures he sees in his life (see p. 35).
13. Why did the Lord give a preview of His second coming in addition to the prophecy in verse 27 (see pp. 36-37)?
14. What are other ways to translate the Greek word translated "kingdom" in Matthew 16:28 (see p. 37)?
15. What are some of the incorrect interpretations of Matthew 16:28? Why are they incorrect (see pp. 37-38)?
16. Where can you find the correct interpretation of Matthew 16:28 (see p. 38)?
17. How did the transfiguration of Christ change Peter's life (see p. 39)?

Pondering the Principles

1. As a Christian, you have great hope for the future because Christ will come in glory to reward you. But what about those who don't know Christ? Read 1 Thessalonians 1:5-10 and 2 Peter 3:7. According to those verses, what does the future hold for unbelievers? Read 2 Corinthians 5:11. What kind of attitude did Paul have toward unbelievers? It is important that you develop that same attitude. If you know of some unbelievers you need to persuade, begin to do so. But remember, don't try to save them yourself. First, ask God to work in their hearts to prepare them to receive the gospel. Be faithful to use the opportunities God gives you for sharing the gospel. Don't presume on God's patience in delaying the return of Christ (2 Peter 3:9-10). Use the time He has given you.

2. The disciples became discouraged when Christ told them about the heavy requirements of discipleship. The same can be true of us. But Matthew 16:27 serves to encourage us as well as the disciples. To begin developing a better perception of Christ's return, look up the following verses: Matthew 24:29-31, Philippians 3:20-21, 1 Thessalonians 4:15-17, 1 John 3:2-3, and Revelation 19-20. Record all your observations of what that time will be like. Meditate on those things and develop a mental picture of the glory to come. Choose the verse most meaningful to you and memorize it for future times of discouragement.

3. Read 2 Peter 3:11. As a result of what you have learned from this study, what kind of person should you be? Record the attitudes and actions you need to develop. Ask God's guidance in implementing them in your life.

3
A Preview of the Second Coming—Part 2

Outline

Review
I. The Principle (16:24)
II. The Paradox (16:25-26)
III. The *Parousia* (16:27)
IV. The Preview (16:28–17:13)
   A. The Promise of the Preview (16:28)

Lesson
   B. The Particulars of the Scene (17:1)
      1. The time (v. 1*a*)
      2. The people (v. 1*b*)
         a) The positive reasons
            (1) They were to be witnesses
            (2) They were closest with Christ
            (3) They were trustworthy leaders
         b) The negative reason
      3. The place (v. 1*c*)
   C. The Proofs of Christ's Deity (17:2-13)
      1. The transformation of the Son (v. 2)
         a) 2 Peter 1:16
         b) John 1:14
         c) Matthew 24:30
         d) Revelation 1:14-16
      2. The testimony of the saints (vv. 3-4)
         a) The verification by the Old Testament saints (v. 3)
             (1) Depicting the representatives
                (*a*) Moses—the giver of the law
                (*b*) Elijah—the guardian of the law

(2) Discussing the plan
    (*a*) Christ's final outcome
    (*b*) The disciples' eventual understanding
  b) The conclusion of the New Testament saints (v. 4)
    (1) The fervency of Peter's conclusion
    (2) The foolishness of Peter's conclusion
  3. The terror of the Father (vv. 5-6)
    a) The cloud of the Father's presence (v. 5*a*)

Conclusion

Review

I. THE PRINCIPLE (16:24; see pp. 10-19)

II. THE PARADOX (16:25-26; see pp. 19-21)

III. THE *PAROUSIA* (16:27; see pp. 21-22, 27-41)

The disciples needed to hear about Christ's future return because it balanced what Christ taught them about dying to self, taking up a cross, and living in obedience (Matt. 16:24). Suffering would be a way of life for them, but it would be wonderfully compensated by Christ's coming in glory.

Matthew: The Presentation of the King

It was Matthew's purpose to present Christ as King. When the King first came into the world He was rejected. But when He returns He will be royally acclaimed and crowned as King of kings and Lord of lords. The fact of the second coming is an important truth in Matthew's gospel (24:29-31; 25:31; 26:63-64).

The second coming of Christ is mentioned in 1,527 passages in the Old Testament and in 319 in the New Testament (René Pache, *The Return of Jesus Christ* [Chicago: Moody, 1955], p. 5). The second coming of Christ is not a message restricted to the New Testament but is well-grounded in the Old Testament as well.

The disciples should have understood that the Messiah would suffer first and then be glorified. But they didn't, so the Lord gave them the promise of verse 27. To insure that they would grasp the importance of that promise, the Lord went beyond the prophecy and promised a preview.

IV. THE PREVIEW (16:28–17:13)

A. The Promise of the Preview (16:28; see pp. 37-40)

The Lord didn't want the disciples to ever doubt the reality of the second coming, so He gave them a glimpse of its glory. It served to balance their understanding of sharing in Christ's sorrows by affirming their participation in His glory. They were encouraged because they now knew that humiliation meant ultimate glory. Romans 8:17 says, "If so be that we suffer with him, that we may be also glorified together." The disciples' hearts were filled with assurance and hope in the midst of great despair.

The Preview Principle

Some people find it difficult to relate the actual transfiguration to the promise given in Matthew 16:28. Another passage of Scripture gives us an example of a similar situation. Acts 2 records the events of the day of Pentecost when the church had its formal birth. On that day, 120 of Christ's followers were gathered in an upper room. In the midst of their time of fellowship and prayer, the Spirit of God came upon them with cloven tongues of fire resting upon each individual (vv. 2-3). They were filled with the Holy Spirit and began to speak languages they did not know (v. 4). The words they spoke told of the wonderful works of God (v. 11). All those things served to announce the arrival of the Spirit of God as He gave official birth to the church.

The people of Jerusalem didn't understand what was happening. Verse 12 says, "They were all amazed, and were perplexed, saying one to another, What meaneth this?" Some of them decided they were drunk (v. 13). But in verse 16 Peter says, "This is that which was spoken through the prophet, Joel." Then from verses 17-21 he quotes from Joel 2:28-32—a passage still to be fulfilled at the second coming: "It shall come to pass in the last days, saith God, I will pour out my Spirit upon all flesh; and your sons and your daughters shall prophesy, and your young men shall see visions, and your old men shall dream dreams; and on my servants and on my handmaidens I will pour out in those days of my Spirit, and they shall prophesy: and I will show wonders in heaven above, and signs in the earth beneath: blood, and fire, and vapor of smoke. The sun shall be turned into darkness, and the moon into blood, before that great notable day of the Lord come; and it shall come to pass that whosoever shall call on the name of the Lord shall be saved" (Acts 2:17-21).

Joel's prophecy is related to the second coming. Notice that everything promised in the prophecy did not happen on the Day of Pentecost. What happened in Acts 2:1-13 was a preview of final kingdom events. The people had a taste of what will happen when Jesus returns. Peter wasn't claiming that all the elements of Joel's prophecy were fulfilled that day, but he was confirming it was a glimpse of final glory. In fact, everything Jesus did in His ministry—all His signs, wonders, and miracles (and those performed by the apostles)—was a taste of His second coming. That's why the writer of Hebrews said the law is "a shadow of good things to come" (Heb. 10:1).

The Near and Far of Prophecy

In the Old Testament it was common for a prophet to couple a prophecy for the near future with a prophecy for the distant future. The near fulfillment enabled the prophets to verify their prophetic role and bolster the people's faith that the distant prophecy would one day come to pass. I believe Jesus was showing Himself to be a trustworthy prophet by predicting His future return in the last days. To prove it, He predicted that some of the disciples wouldn't die until they saw Him in His regal majesty. Thus, when the near prophecy happened, they could trust Him for His future return.

B. The Particulars of the Scene (17:1)

1. The time (v. 1*a*)

"After six days."

Luke 9:28 says it was about eight days. Matthew was probably referring to the exact time whereas Luke was speaking in general terms. Matthew may have been referring to the number of days between the promise and its fulfillment, while Luke may have been including the day of the promise and the day of the fulfillment. There is no contradiction between the two gospels.

2. The people (v. 1*b*)

"Jesus taketh Peter, James, and John, his brother."

Those three disciples were the most intimate with our Lord. Along with Andrew, they were the first to be gathered to His side (Matt. 4:18-22; John 1:40-42). Jesus drew the three of them away from the rest of the disciples. Why did He do that?

a) The positive reasons

(1) They were to be witnesses

Jesus needed witnesses to see His glory. Deuteronomy 19:15 established the principle that any testimony was to be confirmed by two or three witnesses. The Lord wanted the display of His glory confirmed by trustworthy witnesses.

(2) They were closest with Christ

Peter, James, and John were Christ's closest disciples. Perhaps they frequently accompanied Him into intimate times of prayer. I don't believe they would have been surprised that Christ asked them along. Mark 5:37 says they were with Him when He raised a young girl from the dead. They accompanied Him into the Garden of Gethsemane on the night He agonized over His coming death (Mark 14:33). It seems proper that those who most intimately knew His sorrow and suffering should share in His glory. And suffer they did: according to tradition Peter was crucified upside down, James was beheaded, and John was exiled. Certainly they deserved to see His glory.

(3) They were trustworthy leaders

They were men of great spiritual report. When it came time to articulate what happened, they would be trusted. They could convince and influence the other disciples.

b) The negative reason

If all the disciples and the crowd had seen the transfiguration, there would have been no way to prevent widespread chaos. The people would have had even a greater desire to see Jesus as their political and military Messiah. To prevent that from happening, Jesus restricted the preview to Peter, James, and John.

3. The place (v. 1c)

"[Jesus] bringeth them up into an high mountain privately."

We don't know which mountain they went up, but it was located somewhere in upper Galilee south of Caesarea Philippi.

After they arrived at their destination, the disciples were soon sleeping (Luke 9:32). While they were sleeping, Jesus was praying (Luke 9:28). We see this same scenario when the Lord poured out His heart to the Father in the Garden of Gethsemane. The disciples were asleep on that occasion also. Jesus rebuked them and said, "Couldest not thou watch one hour?" (Mark 14:37). Luke 22:45 tells us they were "sleeping for sorrow." When people are depressed they often find they want to sleep. Unfortunately, some people become so depressed that they want to sleep for good, so they take their lives. Some people take sleeping pills so they can escape from their problems. Perhaps the disciples slept because it was the only way to deal with their sorrow. The same thing might have been true on the mount of transfiguration. Only a few days before, Jesus predicted He would be killed and that they would follow Him by taking up the cross (Matt. 16:21, 24). They often viewed their circumstances in the worst light. On one occasion Thomas said, "Let us also go, that we may die with him" (John 11:16).

When the three disciples came out of their sleep, an incredible thing happened unlike anything that has ever happened in the history of the world.

C. The Proofs of Christ's Deity (17:2-13)

In the events that follow are five proofs that Jesus is the King of glory, the Messiah, the Christ, the Son of the living God. The disciples needed that affirmation, and so do we.

1. The transformation of the Son (v. 2)

"[Jesus] was transfigured [Gk., *metamorphoō*] before them; and his face did shine like the sun, and his raiment was as white as the light."

Jesus was totally changed before the three disciples. The Greek root of *metamorphoō* is *morphē*, which refers to form. His form was totally changed. The glory of God was unveiled, radiating from the inside of Christ outward. He was like a supernatural light bulb. The light from within Him was as brilliant as the sun.

The scene leaves little doubt regarding who Christ is. Whenever God, who is spirit (John 4:24), chose to manifest His invisible essence in the Old Testament, He did so as light. In Exodus He manifested Himself in a pillar of fire and a cloud.

a) 2 Peter 1:16—"We have not followed cunningly devised fables when we made known unto you the

49

power and coming of our Lord Jesus Christ, but were eyewitnesses of his majesty."

b) John 1:14—"We beheld his glory, the glory as of the only begotten of the Father, full of grace and truth."

c) Matthew 24:30—"They shall see the Son of Man coming in the clouds of heaven with power and great glory" (cf. Matt. 25:30).

d) Revelation 1:14-16—The apostle John gave the following description of Jesus Christ in his vision: "His head and his hair were white like wool, as white as snow; and his eyes were like a flame of fire; and his feet like fine bronze, as if they burned in a furnace; and his voice like the sound of many waters. And he had in his right hand seven stars; and out of his mouth went a sharp two-edged sword; and his countenance was as the sun shineth in its strength."

When Christ came into the world, He used the veil of humanity to cloak His divine nature. The body is a wall that veils one's inner nature. But when Christ pulled back the veil, the blazing glory of God became visible. That's what the three disciples saw, and that's what we see in this text. The transfiguration leaves no doubt about who Christ is. So don't let anyone tell you Jesus isn't God.

2. The testimony of the saints (vv. 3-4)

a) The verification by the Old Testament saints (v. 3)

"Behold, there appeared unto them Moses and Elijah talking with him."

Luke 9:31 says Moses and Elijah "appeared in glory." They were encompassed by Christ's glory. Why did Moses and Elijah appear?

(1) Depicting the representatives

(a) Moses—the giver of the law

Moses is synonymous with the Old Testament. In fact, the Old Testament sometimes is referred to as Moses and the prophets. The law is called the law of Moses. This great man of God was raised in the court of the king of Egypt. He was exiled to the fields and flocks of Midian, and there learned how to be a humble servant of God. God chose him to confront the Egyptians and lead the people of Israel out of that land through the Sinai wilderness to the borders of the Promised Land. Moses was perhaps the greatest leader who ever lived. He coordinated two million people in a forty-year trek in the desert. At a time when Israel had no king, he was their authority. At a time when they had no prophets, he spoke for God. At a time when they had no priest, he led them to God. Moses served Israel as king, priest, and prophet. He was a leader among leaders. Beyond that, Moses was the agent of the Ten Commandments—the instrument through whom God gave the law, which expressed His will and revealed His character.

(b) Elijah—the guardian of the law

Only one man in the Old Testament could stand with Moses, and that was Elijah, who fought against the nation's idolatry. Moses gave the law; Elijah guarded the law. He was zeal personified. He had courage—he spoke words of bold and profound judgment. He had a heart for God. He had miraculous power (1 Kings 17-22; 2 Kings 1-2). Every prophet should be like Elijah.

Moses and Elijah represent the law and the prophets, which is the Old Testament. Their presence at the transfiguration of Christ is the affirmation of the law and the prophets to the deity of Christ. Jesus said He came to fulfill the law and the prophets (Matt. 5:17). The presence of Moses and Elijah confirms that He did.

(2) Discussing the plan

Matthew 17:3 says Moses and Elijah were talking with Jesus. Luke 9:31 tells us what they were talking about: they "spoke of his decease [departure] which he should accomplish at Jerusalem." They were talking about Christ's death.

(a) Christ's final outcome

The Greek word translated "decease" (*exodos*) means "final outcome." They were talking about His death on the cross as an *exodos*—a departure. Just as the Exodus under Moses delivered the people from the bondage of Egypt, so the exodus of Christ's death would deliver His people from the bondage of sin.

(b) The disciples' eventual understanding

The one element the disciples couldn't understand about the messianic program was the death of Christ. But the presence of Moses and Elijah as representatives of the law and the prophets showed that God's plan was still on schedule—that Christ's eventual death in Jerusalem was part of that plan. What an important conversation for the disciples to hear! That enabled Peter to declare on the Day of Pentecost that the Lord was "delivered by the determinate counsel and foreknowledge of God" (Acts 2:23).

Christ didn't die as a well-meaning patriot who got in over His head; He was ordained to die before the foundation of the world. His death was as much a part of God's plan as His second coming, and it was vital for the disciples to know that.

The disciples were frightened by what they saw (Mark 9:6). Yet their fear was mingled with a sense of awe—they couldn't help but be thrilled. Often in a state of great emotion we don't know what to say. Such was the case for Peter.

b) The conclusion of the New Testament saints (v. 4)

"Then answered Peter, and said unto Jesus, Lord, it is good for us to be here; if thou wilt, let us make here three booths; one for thee, and one for Moses, and one for Elijah."

(1) The fervency of Peter's conclusion

Peter didn't want this experience to end. The phrase "Lord, it is good" means Peter perceived being there as excellent. It was the best thing that ever happened to him. It is hard to know what the motive was for Peter's request, but he loved what he was experiencing. In the ambivalence of his thrill and terror, he made the suggestion. Luke 9:33 says he made the statement not knowing what he was saying.

(2) The foolishness of Peter's conclusion

Matthew 17:5 says, "While [Peter] yet spoke, behold, a bright cloud overshadowed them; and, behold, a voice out of the cloud, which said, This is my beloved Son, in whom I am well pleased; hear ye him." God was telling Peter to keep quiet—it was not the right time for stupid suggestions. But what was wrong with what Peter said? His attitude wasn't wrong, but there was something foolish about his request. Peter didn't understand two things: first, he didn't realize that he had experienced a preview only. He still had to go down the mountain and live through suffering and hardship. The Messiah still had to suffer and die. Second, Peter didn't understand that Jesus, Moses, and Elijah can't be given equal treatment. When Peter offered his suggestion, Moses and Elijah were departing from Jesus (Luke 9:33).

The appearance of Moses and Elijah was temporary because their purpose was to salute their divine successor—the One who fulfilled the law and the prophets—and then to leave Him alone in the glory of unchallenged supremacy. To build booths for all three didn't fit God's plan. Peter simply didn't know what he was talking about.

3. The terror of the Father (vv. 5-6)

   a) The cloud of the Father's presence (v. 5a)

   "While he yet spoke, behold, a bright cloud overshadowed them."

   The Bible has many references to white clouds, and invariably God is present in them. In Revelation 14:14-16 John says, "I looked and, behold, a white cloud, and upon the cloud one sat, like the Son of man, having on his head a golden crown, and in his hand a sharp sickle. And another angel came out of the temple, crying with a loud voice to him that sat on the cloud, Thrust in thy sickle, and reap; for the time is come for thee to reap; for the harvest of the earth is ripe. And he that sat on the cloud thrust in his sickle on the earth, and the earth was reaped." That's a picture of Jesus coming in glory on a white cloud to judge the earth.

   The cloud descended and a voice came out of it saying, "This is my beloved Son, in whom I am well pleased; hear ye him. And when the disciples heard it, they fell on their face, and were very much afraid" (Matt. 17:5-6). God was there. In addition to the testimony of the Old Testament saints and the transformed Son is the testimony of the Father: "This is my beloved Son."

Conclusion

Do you have any doubt about who Jesus Christ is? I hope not. Our response should be like that of Peter, James, and John. We should be thrilled beyond words to be in His presence, yet at the same time be afraid. That divine tension ought to exist in every Christian's life. We delight in His mercy and grace and are in awe of His holiness and judgment. As we walk in obedience, we know the excellence of His presence. When we walk in disobedience, we experience the terror of it.

Focusing on the Facts

1. What was Matthew's purpose for his gospel (see p. 44)?
2. How does Acts 2:1-13 relate to Matthew 16:28–17:13 (see pp. 45-46)?
3. Explain the significance of near and future fulfillment in prophecy (see p. 46).
4. Why did Jesus take only Peter, James, and John with Him up into the mountain (see pp. 47-48)?
5. Why might the disciples have fallen asleep while Jesus prayed (Luke 22:45; see pp. 48-49)?
6. Explain what is meant by transfiguration (Matt. 17:2; see p. 49).
7. How did God often manifest His essence in the Old Testament (see p. 49)?
8. What does the revealed glory of Christ prove about Him (see p. 50)?
9. Give a brief description of the life and ministry of both Moses and Elijah (see p. 51).
10. Why did Moses and Elijah appear with Christ in His glory? What do they represent (see pp. 51-52)?
11. What did Moses and Elijah talk about with Christ? What is significant about that conversation (see p. 52)?
12. What did the conversation teach the disciples about God's plan (see p. 52)?
13. Why was Peter's request in Matthew 17:4 considered foolish (see p. 53)?
14. Why was the appearance of Moses and Elijah temporary (see p. 54)?
15. What is the biblical significance of the presence of white clouds (see p. 54)?
16. What is the divine tension that ought to exist in every Christian's life (see pp. 54-59)?

Pondering the Principles

1. The disciples had difficulty in understanding that Christ's death was an integral part of God's redemptive plan. Through various means and situations, God continued to teach them about it until they finally understood. How do you view God's plan as it relates to you? Do you see yourself as an important tool in God's hands, or do you merely thank God for your salvation and continue living your own life without considering how He wants you to serve Him? Read Matthew 28:19-20 and Acts 1:8. How do you fit into God's redemptive plan? Be honest in your appraisal. You may not be called to train people for evangelism or to be an evangelistic speaker, but you can have an impact in bringing people to Christ in more ways than you think. Be sensitive to the opportunities the Lord gives you to participate in His redemptive plan for the world.

2. When the three disciples experienced the glory of Christ on the mountain, Peter failed to realize that he needed to return to the valley of daily life and the hardships it can involve. Perhaps you have attended a retreat or special seminar that left you with that mountain top "high." Yet when you returned to your daily routine, you left behind much of what you learned. Review Matthew 16:24. As a believer you must be realistic about what Christ has called you to do. As you examine that verse, determine what practical steps you need to take to die to self, take up your cross, and live in obedience to Christ. Prayerfully consider how God wants you to start implementing those things in your life.

4
A Preview of the Second Coming—Part 3

Outline

Introduction
A. The Light of God
B. The Light of Christ
C. The Light of Heaven

Review
I. The Principle (16:24)
II. The Paradox (16:25-26)
III. The *Parousia* (16:27)
IV. The Preview (16:28–17:13)
    A. The Promise of the Preview (16:28)
    B. The Particulars of the Scene (17:1)
    C. The Proofs of Christ's Deity (17:2-13)
        1. The transformation of the Son (v. 2)
        2. The testimony of the saints (vv. 3-4)
            a) The verification of the Old Testament saints (v. 3)
            b) The conclusion of the New Testament saints (v. 4)
                (1) The fervency of Peter's conclusion
                (2) The foolishness of Peter's conclusion

Lesson
                (3) The framework of Peter's conclusion
                    (a) Anticipating the kingdom
                    (b) Seeing the glory
                    (c) Redeeming the people
                    (d) Commemorating the wandering
                    (e) Fulfilling the prophecy
        3. The terror of the Father (vv. 5-6)
            a) The cloud of the Father's presence (v. 5a)
            b) The context of the disciples' fear (v. 6)

Introduction

A. The Light of God

God is spirit and therefore is invisible. Luke 24:39 says, "A spirit hath not flesh and bones." God has no form. When God revealed Himself in the Old Testament, He chose to reveal Himself as a blazing light. In Exodus 33:18 Moses says, "Show me thy glory," and God allowed him to see in part His glory, which had a visible effect on Moses' face (Ex. 34:29-35). When the Tabernacle, the symbol of God's presence, was built, "a cloud covered the tent of the congregation, and the glory of the Lord filled the tabernacle. And Moses was not able to enter into the tent of the congregation, because the cloud abode thereon" (Ex. 40:34-35). When it was time for the people to travel in the wilderness, the glory of God would go up into the sky as a cloud by day and a pillar of fire by night (vv. 36-38). When the people came into the Promised Land and built the Temple, "the glory of the Lord . . . filled the house of the Lord" (1 Kings 8:11).

B. The Light of Christ

In the gospels, God reveals Himself in Jesus Christ as light veiled by human flesh. Jesus Christ was the Shekinah of God. Scripture tells us that when Jesus returns He will come in glory (Matt. 24:30). Jesus Christ is revealed as light. He even said, "I am the light of the world; he that followeth me shall not walk in darkness, but shall have the light of life" (John 8:12).

C. The Light of Heaven

Revelation 21 gives us the details of the eternal heaven and the holy city—the new Jerusalem, the eternal habitation of the saints. Verse 23 says, "The city had no need of the sun, neither of the moon, to shine in it; for the glory of God did light it, and the Lamb is the lamp of it." In heaven Jesus is the lamp containing the light of the glory of God.

When Jesus lived on the earth, His glory was veiled within Him. But in heaven it will be unveiled. When Jesus wanted to reveal Himself as He really is, He pulled back the veil of His flesh and revealed the Shekinah of God.

Review

I. THE PRINCIPLE (16:24; see pp. 10-19)

II. THE PARADOX (16:25-26; see pp. 19-21)

III. THE *PAROUSIA* (16:27; see pp. 21-22, 27-41)

IV. THE PREVIEW (16:28–17:13)

A. The Promise of the Preview (16:28; see pp. 37-40, 45-46)

B. The Particulars of the Scene (17:1; see pp. 47-49)

C. The Proofs of Christ's Deity (17:2-13)

1. The transformation of the Son (v. 2; see pp. 49-50)

2. The testimony of the saints (vv. 3-4)

   a) The verification of the Old Testament saints (v. 3; see pp. 50-53)

   b) The conclusion of the New Testament saints (v. 4)

      (1) The fervency of Peter's conclusion (see p. 53)

      (2) The foolishness of Peter's conclusion (see p. 54)

Lesson

(3) The framework of Peter's conclusion

In the midst of the testimony from Moses and Elijah in Matthew 17:3, Peter says, "Lord, it is good for us to be here; if thou wilt, let us make here three booths; one for thee, and one for Moses, and one for Elijah" (v. 4). I believe Peter had some reasons for making that suggestion.

(a) Anticipating the kingdom

As Peter and the rest of the disciples followed Jesus, they anticipated the coming of the kingdom. After all, when you follow the King you expect to see His kingdom. The Old Testament said the Messiah would come, make things right, and then reign in the kingdom. After Christ's resurrection, they still anticipated its immediate establishment, asking, "Lord, wilt thou at this time restore again the kingdom to Israel?" (Acts 1:6). To them, every moment might be the right time. On one occasion James and John sent their mother to make this request: "Grant that these, my two sons, may sit, the one on thy right hand, and the other on the left, in thy kingdom" (Matt. 20:21).

(*b*) Seeing the glory

Peter had just heard an amazing prophecy. In Matthew 16:27-28 Jesus says, "The Son of man shall come in the glory of his Father. . . . There are some standing here, who shall not taste of death, till they see the Son of man coming in his kingdom." When you combine that prophecy, Peter's anticipation, and the transfiguration he just witnessed, what is the logical conclusion? That prophecy would soon come to pass. But Peter didn't understand that what he saw was only a preview of something that has yet to occur.

(*c*) Redeeming the people

Peter heard Moses and Elijah having a conversation with Jesus about His impending death (Gk., *exodos*, "departure"). Moses led the Exodus, and in Deuteronomy 18:15 he says, "The Lord thy God will raise up unto thee a Prophet from the midst of thee, of thy brethren, like unto me." Moses was referring to another Prophet who would lead another exodus. The people of Israel, including the disciples, were looking for another deliverer, but He was different from what they expected. As Moses led the people out of Egypt into the Promised Land, the Jews of Jesus' time were looking for a deliverer to lead them out from under Roman bondage into freedom. But God had planned a deliverance out of sin into righteousness—from death to life. When Peter heard Jesus talking about His exodus,

I'm sure he thought Christ was the greater prophet who would lead them out from under Roman bondage. Peter also knew that Elijah was to be the forerunner of the Messiah. So when both Elijah and Moses were talking about Christ's exodus, he must have thought that deliverance was going to occur right then.

(d) Commemorating the wandering

It is thought that the transfiguration of Christ occurred in the month of Tishri, which is six months from Passover. Jesus was crucified at Passover. During the month of Tishri the Jews celebrated the feast of Tabernacles, or the feast of Booths. At the time of the transfiguration, it is likely the people were celebrating the feast in Jerusalem. The feast of Tabernacles commemorates the wandering in the wilderness. After God delivered His people out of Egypt, they lived in tabernacles until God led them into the Promised Land. The feast is a memorial to God for preserving His redeemed people in the wilderness. But Peter, James, John, and Jesus weren't at the feast. Peter knew the importance of attending the feast of Tabernacles—all male Jews were required to go every year. Perhaps Peter thought they ought to have their own feast, especially since Moses was present and could give them the best insight into it. After all, the feast did commemorate the Exodus, and they were about to enter into another exodus. In Peter's mind the timing was perfect.

(e) Fulfilling the prophecy

Zechariah 14 tells us about Jesus' return to set up His kingdom. Verse 9 says, "The Lord shall be king over all the earth; in that day shall there be one Lord, and his name one." Verse 16 adds: "It shall come to pass that every one that is left of all the nations which came against Jerusalem shall even go up from year to year to worship the King, the Lord of hosts, and to keep the feast of tabernacles." There will be a thousand years in the millennial kingdom, which means they will keep the feast a thousand times. Verses 18-19 say, "The Lord will smite the nations that come not up to keep the feast of tabernacles. This shall be the punishment of Egypt, and the punishment of all nations that come not up to keep the feast of tabernacles."

Only one of the traditional week-long feasts will be kept in the kingdom, and that's the feast of Tabernacles. Passover and Communion will also be remembered (Luke 22:16, 18), but they didn't last all week. Those three celebrations are pictures of redemption. Because Peter assumed the Millennium was beginning on account of the transfiguration, he thought they should keep the feast of Tabernacles.

In spite of all the reasons Peter may have had for wanting to build booths and celebrating the feast of Tabernacles, Luke 9:33 says he didn't know what he was saying. He didn't realize that what he saw was only a preview of the kingdom—he had not yet understood the need to suffer first. According to 1 Peter 1:11, even the prophets did not understand why the Messiah had to suffer before being glorified. Peter obviously didn't listen to the specifics of the conversation between Jesus, Moses, and Elijah. If he had, he would have heard that Christ's exodus would occur at Jerusalem—the same place our Lord previously predicted as the location for His death and resurrection (Matt. 16:21). I don't believe Peter listened to that prophecy either—he heard only the part about Christ's death and not the part about His resurrection. In both cases, his reasoning was wrong.

3. The terror of the Father (vv. 5-6)

   a) The cloud of the Father's presence (v. 5*a*; see p. 54)

   "While he [Peter] yet spoke, behold, a bright cloud overshadowed them."

   b) The context of the disciples' fear (v. 6)

   "When the disciples heard it [God's voice], they fell on their face, and were very much afraid."

   (1) The reason for fear

   Why are people afraid in the presence of God? Because He is infinitely holy, and men are hopelessly sinful. We feel naked when exposed to His holiness. Genesis 3:7-10 tells us that when Adam and Eve sinned, "they knew that they were naked; and they sewed fig leaves together, and made themselves aprons. And they heard the voice of the Lord God walking in the garden in the cool of the day: and Adam and his wife hid themselves from the presence of the Lord God among the trees of the garden. And the Lord God called unto Adam, and said unto him, Where art thou? And he said, I heard thy voice in the garden, and I was afraid, because I was naked; and I hid myself." Adam and Eve experienced shame because they knew their sin had been exposed. In the presence of holy God sinners will always feel they need to hide. And that is how the disciples felt when they fell flat on the ground after hearing God's voice.

   (2) The examples of fear

   (*a*) Gideon—When Gideon perceived that he was having a conversation with the angel of the Lord (probably Christ in a pre-incarnate appearance), he said, "Alas, O Lord God! For I have seen [the] angel of the Lord face to face. And the Lord said unto him, Peace be unto thee; fear not: thou shalt not die" (Judg. 6:22-

23). He thought he would die having seen God.

(*b*) Manoah—After watching the angel of the Lord ascend into heaven, Manoah told his wife, "We shall surely die, because we have seen God" (Judg. 13:22).

(*c*) Isaiah—When Isaiah saw God he said, "Woe is me! For I am undone . . . for mine eyes have seen the King, the Lord of Hosts" (Isa. 6:5).

(*d*) Daniel—When Daniel saw a vision of the glory of God, he said, "My comeliness was turned into corruption, and I retained no strength. . . . When I heard the voice of his words, then was . . . my face toward the ground" (Dan. 10:8-9).

(*e*) Habakkuk—After hearing God the prophet said, "My belly trembled, my lips quivered at the voice; rottenness entered into my bones, and I trembled in myself" (Hab. 3:16).

c) The contents of the Father's testimony (v. 5*b*)

"This is my beloved Son, in whom I am well pleased; hear ye him."

(1) The essence of the relationship

When God said, "This is my Son," He was referring to the essence of their relationship. Christ is God's Son in the sense that a son is of the same essence as his father—like produces like.

(2) The love of the relationship

God also called Christ his "beloved Son." There is not only an essential relationship between them but also a love relationship.

65

(3) The obedience of the relationship

God then said, "In whom I am well pleased." Everything Jesus did was according to the divine plan. That was important for Peter to hear because he often second-guessed the Lord on His decisions. Christ is obedient and faithful to God. He went to Jerusalem to suffer and die because that was God's plan. God was well pleased with Christ for His obedience.

(4) The authority of the relationship

At the end of verse 5 God says, "Hear ye him." God was confirming that when Christ said, "If any man will come after me, let him deny himself, and take up his cross, and follow me" (Matt. 16:24), the disciples should listen and obey Him. God not only confirmed the deity of Jesus Christ but also testified to the authority of His words.

4. The tapestry of the scene (vv. 7-9)

a) The purpose of the transfiguration

In Matthew 16:28 Jesus tells the disciples that some of them would see "the Son of man coming in his kingdom." How did the transfiguration fulfill that? By providing us with a miniature picture of the second coming.

(1) The subject

Christ is the center of this picture, and He will be the center of the second coming. When Christ comes, He will come in power and glory (Matt. 24:30). We see Him in power and glory in His transfiguration.

(2) The backdrop

Zechariah 14:4 says Christ's "feet shall stand in that day upon the Mount of Olives." Jesus took the three disciples up into a high mountain to witness the transfiguration. The preview happened on a mountain, and so will the real thing.

(3) The audience

When Jesus returns in glory, He will come to gather together His people. Peter, James, and John were present with Christ when He was glorified. They represent the saints who will be on earth when Christ returns. But there's another dimension: when Christ returns, He will be accompanied by saints who previously were gathered together to be with Christ. They are represented by Moses and Elijah, who appeared with Christ in His glory. Further, we know Moses died because there was a dispute over his body (Jude 9). But Elijah never died—God took him up into heaven in a divine chariot. So Moses represents saints who have already died, and Elijah represents the saints who will be raptured.

All the parts of the second coming were present at the preview. No wonder Peter said, "We have not followed cunningly devised fables when we made known unto you the power and coming of our Lord Jesus Christ, but were eyewitness of his majesty" (2 Pet. 1:16).

b) The end of the transfiguration (vv. 7-8)

"Jesus came and touched them, and said, Arise, and be not afraid. And when they had lifted up their eyes, they saw no man, except Jesus only."

The preview was over. The kingdom wasn't beginning—it was just a preview. The three disciples had seen the Son of Man in His royal majesty. They were so traumatized by it that they never would forget. Years later when people questioned the reality of Christ's return, Peter could say, "The day of the Lord will come like a thief in the night" (2 Pet. 3:10). The transfiguration was an indelible experience. But it ended because it wasn't yet time for glory. Before glory there must be suffering.

c) The response to the transfiguration (v. 9)

What would your reaction be to that scene? I know I probably would have said, "I've got to get down to the valley and tell Andrew and the others. We'll be the only people who can say we have met Moses and Elijah!"

(1) The delay of declaration (v. 9*a*)

"As they came down from the mountain, Jesus charged them, saying, Tell the vision [Gk., *horama*, "spectacle"] to no man."

That command rivals Zacharias's problem. When the angel Gabriel predicted the birth of John the Baptist, Zacharias didn't believe him (Luke 1:18). As a result, the Lord struck him dumb so that he couldn't tell anyone he was going to have a son (v. 20). That would be hard on any father, and it was hard for the three disciples.

More than once Jesus told people not to tell anyone about something He did (e.g., Matt. 16:20). That's because the people of Israel wanted a political Messiah who would defeat the Romans. Their misguided intentions and expectations would have only confused the scene. If the three disciples were to announce that they had seen the majesty of Christ, the people would have tried to get Jesus to overthrow the Romans. They had done so at least once before (John 6:15).

(2) The day of declaration (v. 9*b*)

"Until the Son of man is raised again from the dead."

If the disciples waited until after the resurrection, the people would know Christ didn't come to conquer the Romans but to conquer death. Jesus is not involved in politics—He is involved in conquering death, sin, and hell. After the resurrection the people could better understand the spiritual reality of Christ's ministry.

5. The truth about the forerunner (vv. 10-13)

   a) The request (v. 10)

   "His disciples asked him, saying, Why then say the scribes that Elijah must first come?"

   The disciples had just seen Elijah, so he was on their mind. They knew him to be the forerunner of the Messiah because Malachi 4:5-6 says, "Behold, I will send you Elijah, the prophet, before the coming of the great and terrible day of the Lord; and he shall turn the heart of the fathers to the children, and the heart of the children to their fathers, lest I come and smite the earth with a curse." Knowing that, they didn't understand why Elijah hadn't come as the forerunner to Christ's ministry. I'm convinced the Jews must have questioned the disciples on this subject: How could Jesus be the Messiah when there had been no appearance of Elijah?

   There were some people who thought Jesus was Elijah. Matthew 16:13-14 says Jesus "asked his disciples, saying, Who do men say that I, the Son of man, am? And they said, Some say that thou art . . . Elijah." Those people thought He could be Elijah preparing for the Messiah but that He couldn't be the Messiah since Elijah hadn't come before Him.

The Scribal Elijah

The scribes didn't just say Elijah had to come first; they embellished the prophecy of Malachi 4:5-6. They believed Elijah would be a great and terrible reformer who would bring holiness out of unholiness and order out of chaos. They believed He would destroy all evil and make everything right so that all the Messiah had to do was take control of what Elijah had accomplished. They saw Elijah as the true restorer.

The disciples wanted to know who and where Elijah was if Christ was the Messiah.

b) The restoration (v. 11)

"Jesus answered and said unto them, Elijah truly shall first come, and restore all things."

Christ declared that Elijah indeed would come and restore all things before the establishment of the kingdom.

c) The rejection (vv. 12-13)

(1) Of John the Baptist (vv. 12a, 13)

"But I say unto you, That Elijah is come already, and they knew him not, but have done unto him whatsoever they desired. . . . Then the disciples understood that he spoke unto them of John the Baptist."

(a) The spirit of Elijah's appearance

John the Baptist is Elijah in the manner prophesied by Malachi the prophet. Malachi wasn't referring to the actual Elijah; he was referring to one who would come in the same manner, style, and mode of operation as Elijah.

The Jews were looking for the literal Elijah. The chief priests asked John the Baptist, "Art thou Elijah? And he saith, I am not" (John 1:21). Some people have a hard time reconciling that with Christ's statement in Matthew 17:12. However, the point is that John was not Elijah himself, but he did come in the spirit and power of Elijah (Luke 1:17). But the people rejected John so he couldn't be the fulfillment of Malachi's prophecy. There yet will be another who will come in the spirit and power of Elijah in fulfillment of that prophecy before Christ's second coming.

(b) The significance of the people's rejection

If the people had received John the Baptist and believed his message, and if they had received the Messiah and allowed Him to set up His kingdom, John the Baptist would have been the fulfillment of the prophecy in Malachi 4:5-6. But when the people refused him by cutting off his head, they eliminated any chance of the immediate fulfillment of that prophecy. As a result, John the Baptist was not the fulfillment of Malachi's prophecy, and another must still come to fulfill it. Luke 1:17 says, "He [John the Baptist] shall go before him [Christ] in the spirit and power of Elijah, to turn the hearts of the fathers to the children, and the disobedient to the wisdom of the just, to make ready a people prepared for the Lord." Matthew 11:13-14 says, "All the prophets and the law prophesied until John. And if ye will receive it, this is Elijah, who was to come." But they didn't receive him.

(c) The support of Christ's deity

The Jews claimed Christ couldn't have been the Messiah because Elijah didn't precede Him, but Jesus said Elijah did precede Him. That is yet another proof that Jesus is the Messiah because Elijah did come before Him. When Christ comes again, He will be preceded by another Elijah.

(2) Of Christ (v. 12*b*)

"Likewise shall also the Son of man suffer of them."

Suffering before the glory is the message of Matthew 16:21–17:13. In Matthew 16:21 Jesus tells the disciples He must suffer and die. In verse 24 He tells them they must deny themselves—die to their desires and sins—and take up a cross. They were going to bear reproach. Christians have been mocked, scorned, and martyred throughout the history of the church. That's the way life often is for true disciples of Christ, but in the future there will be glory. Christ told the disciples He would suffer (Matt. 16:24-25) and concluded on that note (Matt. 17:12). But in between He gave them a glimpse of His future glory. We would do well to remember the words of the apostle Paul to Timothy: "If we suffer, we shall also reign with him" (2 Tim. 2:12). That's our great hope. What small measure of suffering we endure in this life is not worthy to be compared with the glory that awaits us in Christ (2 Cor. 4:17).

Focusing on the Facts

1. How did God manifest Himself in the Old Testament (see pp. 58-59)?
2. What will be the light in heaven (Rev. 21:23; see p. 59)?
3. What motivated Peter to want to put up booths at the transfiguration of Christ? Explain each reason (see pp. 60-63).
4. What did Peter misunderstand about the type of deliverance God planned to accomplish through Christ (see pp. 61-62)?
5. What does the feast of Tabernacles commemorate (see p. 62)?
6. What part of the conversation between Jesus, Moses, and Elijah did Peter fail to understand? What prophecy did that conversation relate to (see p. 63)?
7. Why are people afraid when in the presence of God (see p. 64)?
8. Describe how certain Old Testament saints behaved when confronted with the presence of God (see pp. 64-65).
9. In Matthew 17:5 God says, "This is my beloved Son, in whom I am well pleased; hear ye him." Explain the significance of that statement (see pp. 65-66).
10. Explain how the transfiguration pictures the second coming (see pp. 66-67).
11. Why did Christ command the three disciples not to tell anyone about what they had seen on the mountain (see p. 68)?
12. When did Christ want the disciples to announce what they had seen on the mountain? Why (Matt. 17:9; see pp. 68-69)?

13. What did the scribes believe Elijah would accomplish as the forerunner to the Messiah? Why did the disciples ask the question in Matthew 17:10 (see p. 69)?
14. In what way can John the Baptist be described as Elijah (see p. 70)?
15. What would have happened had the people received John the Baptist and believed his message? What happened as a result of their rejecting him (see p. 71)?
16. How does the appearance of John the Baptist as Christ's forerunner support the deity of Christ (see p. 71)?

Pondering the Principles

1. What kind of sensitivity do you have toward your sin? Do you see it as something that offends God, or do you see it merely as something you need to confess but don't really try to eliminate? When the disciples were in the presence of the Lord, they fell to the ground. What is your reaction when you are convicted of your sin? Remember, God knows all we think, say, and do. Take this time to humble yourself before God. Ask Him to show you your sin. Confess it, and ask Him to help you eliminate it from your life. Repent of that sin, and covenant with God to be obedient to Him in all areas of your life.

2. At the end of Matthew 17:5 God tells the three disciples to listen to Jesus. Do you listen to Jesus? Do you study the words of our Lord in Scripture with the intent of obeying them, or do you listen just for the purpose of learning? Read James 1:22-25. What kind of hearer are you? What kind of hearer should you be? The next time you read or study God's Word, determine what God wants you to do. Then do it. Make sure you apply something to your life each time you open the Bible.

Scripture Index

Topical Index